Making Amigos in the Land of Windmills

Barbara Youree

Beacon Hill Press of Kansas City
Kansas City, Missouri

Copyright 1999
by Beacon Hill Press of Kansas City.

Printed in the United States of America.

ISBN 083-411-7657

Cover Design: Ted Ferguson
Illustrator: Keith Alexander
Editor: Bruce Nuffer
Editorial Assistant: Alicia Hilton

Unless otherwise indicated, all Scripture quotations are taken from the
Holy Bible, New International Version® (NIV®). Copyright © 1973, 1978, 1984
by International Bible Society. Used by permission of Zondervan
Publishing House. All rights reserved.

Note: This book is based on a true story. It is part of the Understanding
Christian Mission, Children's Mission Education curriculum. It is de-
signed for use in Year 4, The Missionary. This study year examines how
missionaries live and how their work impacts the lives of others.

10   9   8   7   6   5   4   3   2   1

CHAPTER 1

Leaving Home

"Why does God want us to move to Amsterdam *[AM-stur-dam]?*" Ryan asked his dad. "You and I can't even speak Dutch." Ryan's mother learned the Dutch language when she was a nurse in the Netherlands.

"Well," said Dad, "you remember we all prayed about moving from Guatemala. We believe God called us to make this change."

"OK, I know we're *supposed* to go, but why? I miss the mountains, the city market, and especially *mis amigos [MEES ah-MEE-gohs]* (my friends)."

"God might have some surprises for us," said Mom. "He probably even has a special job for you."

"Yeah, right," laughed Ryan, "I'm probably supposed to teach little Dutch kids to sing 'Jesus Loves Me' in Spanish."

"Who knows?" Dad asked as the family bumped along in the old truck. Soon they would get on an airplane to fly all the way to Amsterdam.

Two Surprises

*R*yan woke up in a small two-room apartment at the missionary base. For a moment he forgot where he was. *Oh, yes, we finally made it to Amsterdam,* he thought. Outside it was barely getting light. Ryan shivered as he pulled on his jeans and gray sweatshirt.

So far he hadn't seen any sunshine here. Worst of all, no kids his age were staying at the base—only toddlers and teenagers.

Ryan had started fourth grade in Guatemala. Until they found a house, he would do his schoolwork with his parents. *It wouldn't be so bad,* he thought, *if I had my own room and some friends.*

✳ ✳ ✳

"*Dag [dak]* (Hi), Sleepyhead," Dad said when Ryan finally showed up at his dad's office with his math book.

"Dag, Pappie [pop-PEE]. That's about all I know in Dutch."

"Me too," said Dad, "but we'll learn. I've got good news and bad news. Which do you want first?"

How could it get much worse? Ryan thought. But out loud he said, "Let's have the bad first."

"About the only way to find a house is to get on a waiting list. In a couple of weeks they will send us the facts about the houses."

"A couple of weeks!" Ryan said, horrified.

"Yes, a couple of weeks. Then we pick out a place. If other families want it, the first on the list gets it. I hear it could take a year or more."

Ryan swallowed hard and tried to keep back tears. "And the good news?"

"Remember that job you said God probably had for you here?"

"Ye—s. You mean about teaching Dutch kids to sing in Spanish? But I was just kidding."

"Well, next Wednesday afternoon, you and Mom will be going to a place where Spanish-speaking kids from South America meet. Their mothers have Bible study on the second floor. And the Kids' Group is on the third floor. Most are about your age, and you can help," explained Dad.

"Great! God must have thought I meant it."

"More likely it was already in His plan," said Dad.

"But won't the kids be in school in the afternoon?"

"No school on Wednesday afternoon in the Netherlands," said Dad.

"Now, that is good news!" said Ryan.

Just then Mom rushed into the room waving a newspaper. "Talk about good news, I may have found a miracle!"

She spread out the newspaper on Dad's desk. "There's an ad here about a three-story row house for rent in a little town near Amsterdam. The secretary said people hardly ever put rent ads in the paper. Isn't that amazing?"

Ryan Pool with parents, Keith and Bobbe Pool,
on the bridge overlooking a canal.

The whole family took a bus out to see it. After a very quick look around, Dad said, "We'll take it."

"Isn't God full of surprises?" asked Mom.

"Two in one day," said Dad. "The Spanish group, and now this. Let's take a walk around our new neighborhood."

"Look, the Netherlands isn't always cloudy!" said Ryan. Sunshine began to glisten on the still water of the canal. They stood on the little bridge of a bicycle path to watch the ducks glide under it. In the distance they could see three windmills.

"What do the windmills do?" asked Ryan.

"The wind turns the sails around," explained Mom. "That makes power to turn the wheels inside. They grind up grain and other things."

"Can you climb up on the platform at the top?" Ryan asked.

"Sure," said Dad, "maybe one day we'll do that."

CHAPTER 3

The Kids' Group

Señora Lopez [sen-YOHR-ah LOH-pez] met them at the security gate. "Your help is an answer to our prayers," she said. *My prayers too,* thought Ryan. At last he could have fun with some other kids.

"They may be a little loud at times. They haven't had much training," she continued. "Most of these Spanish-speaking people are living here illegally. Even the children fear being discovered."

"What happens if they are caught?" Ryan asked.

"They are sent back to their own countries. They will have a life of poverty and probably no schooling," she said, shaking her head. "You can go on up to the third floor. Two girls are already waiting for you."

Easier said than done. In their Guatemalan town, there were no two-story build-

ings. Here all the buildings were tall and narrow with skinny, winding stairs. Climbing the stairs with their guitar, Bible posters, and other stuff was not easy.

* * *

Ryan liked leading the Spanish songs while Mom played the guitar. The children most enjoyed the songs with actions. They liked "Deep and Wide" and "If You're Saved and You Know It, Stomp Your Feet." One boy, Carlos, liked to show off. He sang extra loud and stomped like he was stepping on bugs. Ryan laughed so hard he couldn't sing. He stopped when his mom frowned at him.

Then Señora Lopez taught a Bible story— the one Jesus told about loving our neighbors. A man was beaten up by robbers. Two church men walked around him on the other side of the road. But a Samaritan, who was from another town, stopped and bandaged up his cuts. He took him on his donkey to an inn for care. That's being a good neighbor. (Luke 10:30-36)

"Now, I want some of you to act out the story," said Señora Lopez. "Let's see if you understood it."

"I'll be the guy who gets beaten," said Carlos, "and Ryan can fix me up." Carlos pulled him to the front.

When the pretend robbers hit Carlos with cardboard sticks, he groaned and fell down. Then he made funny faces and rolled around. After the two "church men" walked by, Ryan rode up on a broom donkey. He tried to be serious as he pretended to bandage his cuts.

But Carlos didn't want to get on the broom donkey. He was having too much fun rolling around and making everyone laugh. This was the most fun Ryan had had in a long time. He thought it would be funny to drag Carlos off to the inn. When he grabbed his foot and started dragging him, the children all jumped up and cheered.

"That's enough," said Mom sternly.

"Let's all sit down and be quiet," said Señora Lopez. "Carlos, you sit here."

"And, Ryan, over here by me," said Mom, not smiling.

Ryan knew he and Carlos had messed up the story. *But Carlos started it*, he thought.

* * *

On the bus going home, Mom said, "Ryan, I brought you along to help teach other children about Jesus."

"Carlos started it," said Ryan weakly. *I came to have fun*, he thought. *What's wrong with that?*

"Carlos doesn't know how to behave. You do," said Mom. "Carlos doesn't have Christian parents to teach him about God."

Ryan sat quietly and looked out the window at the canals and the faraway windmills. He thought about how the play started fine. A little fun was probably OK. He liked Carlos. They both enjoyed joking. But he knew better than to change the story by dragging Carlos across the floor—even if it was funny.

What would it be like not to have Christian parents? he thought. *What if I didn't know how to talk to God about stuff?*

"I'm sorry, Mom," Ryan finally said. "I'll be good next time."

"I'll count on it," said Mom, giving him a hug around the shoulders.

Ryan thought a lot about Carlos that week. He decided to do something to help him next time.

CHAPTER 4

How Ryan Helps

Where's Carlos?" asked Ryan the next Wednesday afternoon. No one knew where Carlos was. Ryan didn't have to work at being good today.

Ryan wrote a Bible verse in Spanish on the board, and he helped teach a new song. Señora Lopez even made cookies for the children. But Ryan missed Carlos.

Another week passed. Ryan forgot all about his decision to help Carlos. When he and his mom returned to the room, several children were drawing on the chalkboard. Carlos was sitting quietly by himself.

When Carlos saw Ryan, he picked up a long handle from a broken toy. He started walking like an old man with a cane. He trembled and talked in a shaky voice. "Co-me he-lp me, Ry-an," he said, making a funny face.

Then he turned the cane into a gun. "Pow, pow, pow," he said as he pointed the stick at the kids at the chalkboard.

"Hey, they're on our side," said Ryan laughing. "Where were you last week?"

Suddenly Carlos got quiet again. "I had to take care of my little sister. . . . My mother didn't come home."

"Your mother didn't come home?" Ryan couldn't believe it.

"She's gone a lot. When she's home she's usually sick from drinking too much alcohol," Carlos said, and pretended to throw up.

"What does your dad do?" asked Ryan, worried.

"Never met the guy. My mother doesn't even know where he is," said Carlos as if he didn't care. "So what?"

It was time to begin. Ryan stood up front by Mom and led the songs. Carlos acted goofy as he sang the ones with motions and clapping. Ryan thought, *How can he act so silly when I know he is worried about his mother?*

Ryan wrote the Bible verse on the chalkboard: . . . *If we ask anything according to his will, he hears us. And if we know that he hears us—whatever we ask—we know that we have what we asked of him* (1 John 5:14-15).

Mom explained how we pray to God about our problems. Señora Lopez told how she did bad things, but several years ago she came to this building and heard Jesus loved her. She prayed to God to change her life. He did. Now she works here, and her two grown sons are pastors in Amsterdam.

Ryan wanted to tell Carlos God could help him and his mother, but he didn't know what to say. In his head he could still hear Carlos acting like an old man saying, *"Co-me he-lp me, Ry-an."* It made him remember he really did want to help his friend.

After the Bible story, everyone got in a circle. Each child was asked to say a sentence prayer, thanking God for something.

Carlos was next to Ryan. "I hate this," he whispered, "I never know what to say."

"Just say the same thing I do," Ryan whispered back.

It was Ryan's turn. He prayed, "Thank You, God, we can ask You for anything and You hear us."

Carlos bowed his head and said, "Thank You, God, we can ask You for anything and You hear us."

＊　＊　＊

When it was over, Mom said, "You boys were really good this afternoon. How would you like to go for a doughnut?"

"Me? Good?" Carlos laughed. "Don't tell anyone. I don't even believe it myself."

"When we go downstairs, ask your mother if you can go with us," said Mom.

"She doesn't come here. She has to take care of my little sister," said Carlos. "But it's OK."

"Then how did you know where to come?" asked Mom.

"I don't know. I guess I was bored one day and saw some kids coming in here. I just followed them," said Carlos. "Señora Lopez said I could stay."

"Your mother can bring your sister with

her if she would like to come," said Mom.

The boys had a good time telling jokes and eating doughnuts. But when Ryan got home, he wished he had done something to help Carlos. He didn't know what to do.

✽ ✽ ✽

At supper that evening, Mom told Dad she was worried about a boy in the Kids' Group named Carlos. "He came by himself. His mother isn't even in the Bible study," she said. Ryan listened closely to see what his dad would say.

"We will pray for him and his mother," said Dad. "You know, praying isn't the least we can do. It's the most."

I guess I did do something, thought Ryan. *I showed him how to pray.*

CHAPTER 5

"What's Wrong?"

Ryan hurried home from school on his bike—across the little bridge over the frozen canal. Wednesday was always his favorite day. No school and he liked going to the afternoon Kids' Group.

School was boring because he didn't know what the teacher was saying. He would have to be in fourth grade again next year. He spoke English at home with his parents, Spanish at the Kids' Group, and tried to learn Dutch at school. It was all very confusing.

"Hi, Mom!" he called, bursting in the front door and hanging his coat on the hook. The wonderful smell of hot peanut sauce, called *sate [sā-TAY]*, greeted him. Dutch kids love it on their French fries.

But he knew something was wrong when he saw his dad home, sitting in the living

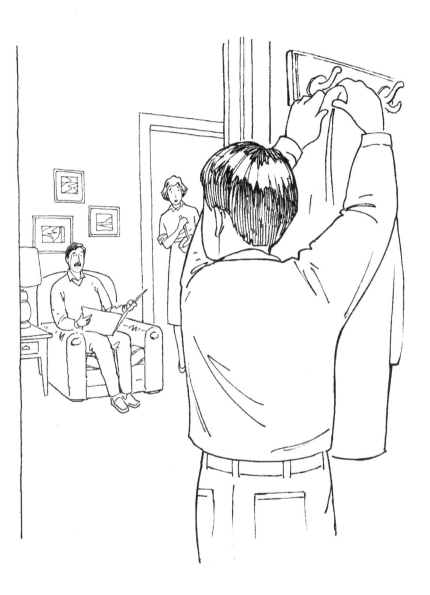

room. Mom stood in the kitchen doorway, holding the saucepan. They both looked worried.

"Come have lunch, Ryan," she said.

After his dad said the blessing, Ryan couldn't wait any longer. "What's wrong?" he asked, looking first at his dad, then his mom.

"There was a police raid last night," Dad began, "in the Spanish district in Amsterdam."

"The police arrested several families," Mom said. "Remember it's illegal for some of them to be here."

Ryan nearly choked on his *sate*-covered French fries.

"Was Carlos arrested?"

"We don't know," his dad answered. "I'm going back to the city after lunch. I'll see what I can find out."

❋   ❋   ❋

Ryan spent the afternoon practicing ice skating on the canal. His dad showed him how last Saturday, but he fell a lot. Then a neighbor lady gave him an old wooden chair.

"Hold on to this next time," she said. "That's how the Dutch kids learn."

The sun was out, and soon he was gliding along the ice, even without the chair. A girl from school joined him for a while. *"Heel goed, [hiel-gyent],"* she said. *That means very good,* Ryan said proudly to himself.

But all he could think about was his only real friend, Carlos. *He may have been sent back to . . . I don't even know where he's from,* thought Ryan.

That evening when Dad came home, he told Ryan, "Señora Lopez and I went to Carlos's apartment. The landlord said they moved, and then he slammed the door in our faces."

CHAPTER 6

True Friends

When the phone rang, it was Dad. He told Mom that Carlos and his family hid in the attic of a friend's house. Last night they came to talk to Señora Lopez. Dad said to take the bus to Amsterdam after lunch—and bring Ryan.

Later that day Dad and Señora Lopez talked and prayed with Carlos's mother. Mom stayed with his little sister. Ryan and Carlos sat upstairs coloring animal pictures.

"Weren't you scared?" Ryan asked.

"Sure. I know some people who got arrested. I don't want to go back to the Dominican Republic."

"Where's that?"

"It's part of an island by South America. We lived with my grandparents. The floor was just dirt. The rain came through the palm-leaf roof. We all had to huddle in the corner—to stay out of the mud."

"Tell me more," said Ryan.

"I don't remember much. Grandmother washed the clothes in the river. I took a bath in the river. That was fun. Then we both spread the clothes out on bushes to dry."

"That's how most people live in Guatemala," said Ryan.

Carlos got very quiet. He seemed to think only about the horse he was coloring. Then he said, "Ryan, do you think . . . does God . . . I mean . . . like, can God really hear people pray?"

"Yes."

"Well, I prayed Mother would stop drinking," said Carlos. "She didn't drink the whole time we stayed in that attic. But then she had two drinks before she came here last night. I *meant* I wanted God to never let her drink again!"

"God knows what you meant," said Ryan.

CHAPTER 7

Finding Home

Ryan was surprised when Carlos's mother walked in with Señora Lopez and his dad. He had always thought she would look sort of mean. Instead, even though her eyes were red from crying, they were large and pretty. Her dark hair was long and wavy, pulled back with a blue ribbon.

She smiled kindly at the boys. "I'm so happy," she said, "Señora Lopez and Ryan's dad have shown me God's love."

Then she hugged Carlos tight. She said, "I promise to be a better mother, Carlos, and stop drinking." Carlos hugged her back.

"You will be living here for a while," said Dad to Carlos.

"The police won't bother you," said Señora Lopez. "I've told them your mother will be working here in the office. I think she can soon be living in the Netherlands legally."

Ryan Pool on the platform of a windmill

"And one more thing," said Dad.

"What's that?" asked Carlos and Ryan together.

"It's time you boys learned more about this country. Saturday both our families are going to visit a Dutch windmill."

"Can we climb up in it?" asked Carlos with a grin.

"Clear to the top! And stand on the platform," promised Dad.

Ryan thought about his friend, about answered prayer—and about how he had always wanted to climb up in a windmill. *I'm glad God brought me here to Amsterdam,* he said to himself. *I'm glad Carlos is* mi amigo.